CARIBOU
OF THE ARCTIC

SARA SWAN MILLER

PowerKiDS
press™
New York

Published in 2009 by The Rosen Publishing Group, Inc.
29 East 21st Street, New York, NY 10010

First Edition

Editor: Amelie von Zumbusch
Book Design: Kate Laczynski
Photo Researcher: Jessica Gerweck

Photo Credits: Cover, back cover, p. 1 © www.istockphoto.com/Paul Loewen; back cover (emperor penguins) © www.istockphoto.com/Bernard Breton; back cover (polar bears) © www.istockphoto.com/Michel de Nijs; back cover (seals), pp. 8, 12 Shutterstock.com; back cover (walruses) © Getty Images; back cover (whales), pp. 4, 10 © Paul Nicklen/Getty Images; p. 6 © Jerry Kobaleno/Getty Images; p. 14 © Johnny Johnson/Getty Images; p. 16 © Wayne R. Bilenduke/Getty Images; p. 18 © Jochem Wijnands/Age Fotostock; p. 20 © Maria Stenzel/Getty Images.

Library of Congress Cataloging-in-Publication Data

Miller, Sara Swan.
   Caribou of the Arctic / Sara Swan Miller. — 1st ed.
      p. cm. — (Brrr! Polar animals)
   Includes index.
   ISBN 978-1-4358-2744-8 (library binding) — ISBN 978-1-4358-3148-3 (pbk.)
ISBN 978-1-4358-3154-4 (6-pack)
   1. Caribou—Arctic regions—Juvenile literature. I. Title.
   QL737.U55M55 2009
   599.65'8—dc22
                                      2008030452

Manufactured in the United States of America

CONTENTS

4

Caribou coats can be dark brown, nearly white,
or a shade of brown somewhere in between.

WHAT ARE CARIBOU?

Caribou are large deer that live in herds in the Far North. A large caribou can stand 5 feet (1.5 m) tall at the shoulder. The only deer that are bigger are elk and moose. The first things most people notice about caribou are their big, branching **antlers**. A male caribou's antlers may be as wide as 4 feet (1 m) across.

Tame caribou that people raise in herds are known as reindeer. They look very much like wild caribou but are a little smaller. People raise reindeer for their meat, milk, and skins.

6

These Peary caribou live on Canada's Axel Heiberg Island.
Peary caribou are one of several subspecies, or kinds, of caribou.

WHERE CAN YOU FIND CARIBOU?

Caribou live up in the Arctic, which is the area around the North Pole. They travel around together over the **tundra**. The tundra is large and flat. Under the tundra's **surface** is a frozen, or icy, **layer** called permafrost, which hardly ever melts. No trees grow on the tundra. Only small plants and **lichen** can be found there. Sometimes caribou drift into the **taiga**, or cool northern forest. Only small trees grow in the taiga.

It is very cold in the Arctic. Caribou have special coats that keep them warm, though. The coats' hairs are hollow and keep the heat in and the cold out.

During the spring and summer, caribou antlers
are covered by hairy skin, called velvet.

WONDERFUL ANTLERS

For the most part, only male deer have antlers. However, both male and female caribou have antlers. The females' antlers are smaller, though. Caribou shed their antlers once a year and grow new ones a few months later. That is a good thing because antlers can get hurt, or their tips can break off.

What is the use of these heavy antlers? Caribou use them to brush snow off the plants they want to eat. Male caribou also use their antlers for fighting. At **mating** time, the males start fighting over the females. The males jab, push, and **wrestle**. The winners get to mate with the females.

These caribou are part of the Bathurst Herd.
This is one of Canada's largest caribou herds.

GREAT HERDS OF CARIBOU

Caribou always travel together in big herds. There may be thousands of caribou in one herd. One herd in Alaska, called the Porcupine Herd, has more than 120,000 caribou! Generally, different herds live apart from each other. In the winter, though, some herds may mix together. Being all together in a herd helps **protect** the caribou from their enemies. There is safety in numbers!

The herds move all the time, searching for fresh food to eat. You might think that with so many caribou all together, there would be fights. However, except at mating time, the caribou get along well.

These caribou are grazing, or eating growing grass.
Caribou eat grass during the spring and summer.

WHAT'S FOR DINNER?

There is not much to eat in the Arctic, but caribou find enough. A big male can weigh as much as 700 pounds (320 kg)! In the winter, caribou eat lichen, dried grasses, and small bushes, such as blueberry bushes. They use their antlers and their big hooves to brush away the snow. In the summer, caribou eat willow leaves, fresh grasses, flowering plants, and mushrooms.

Like other deer, caribou have no top front teeth. Instead, they have a leathery pad. They take a plant between the pad and their lower teeth and pull hard.

These members of the Porcupine Herd are migrating across a group of mountains, called the Brooks Range.

CARIBOU ON THE MOVE

Every year, caribou herds travel hundreds of miles (km) from their winter feeding grounds to their summer feeding grounds. This is called migration.

The summer feeding grounds are where female caribou raise their young. The whole herd spends the summer there, too. In the fall, male and female caribou mate. Finally, in late fall, the herd begins the long trip south for the winter. When the snow begins to melt in May, female caribou start traveling north. They may travel 400 miles (644 km) along well-traveled trails. Their sharp hooves keep them from slipping on the rocks. The males and **yearlings** follow a few weeks later.

Though they will sometimes have two babies, mother caribou most often have just one calf at a time.

CARIBOU CALVES

Caribou calves are often born during the migration north. When they are born, the babies fall to the ground. Just a few minutes later, the calves struggle to their feet. After a few hours, they can run with the herd. They can swim strongly soon after birth. These skills help protect the calves from enemies.

The calves weigh only about 13 pounds (6 kg) when they are born. In only two weeks, they weigh two times that amount. Calves grow fast because their mothers' milk is very rich. Calves stay close to their mothers and nurse often. Soon, the young caribou start eating leaves and buds.

Polar bears, such as this one, sometimes catch caribou. However, polar bears most often eat seals.

WATCH OUT, CARIBOU!

Caribou have many enemies. Wolves, grizzly bears, and wild cats, called lynx, all like the taste of caribou. Coyotes and golden eagles hunt the newborn young. Sometimes, caribou will try to drive their enemies away by kicking out with their sharp hooves or jabbing with their antlers. The best thing they can do, though, is to run away on their long, strong legs.

In the summer, thousands of **mosquitoes** bite caribou and suck their blood. Flies lay their eggs on caribou's backs, too. It is painful! To escape these pests, caribou run away to windy hilltops or dive into rivers, where flies and mosquitoes cannot reach them.

The Nenets are one of the Arctic peoples who herd
reindeer. The Nenets live in northwestern Russia.

PEOPLE AND REINDEER

In Lapland and other northern places, some people herd reindeer. These people follow the herds from place to place across the tundra. This herding has been going on for at least 2,000 years. The reindeer are still half wild, but they are tame enough to let the herders milk them.

Reindeer are very important to these people. They eat the reindeer's meat and drink their milk. Reindeer skins make warm clothing that protects the people from the biting cold. They also use the skins to make tents and blankets. Sometimes these Arctic people even use reindeer to pull their **sleds**!

WHAT WILL HAPPEN TO THE CARIBOU?

Today, there are fewer caribou than there were 200 years ago. During the nineteenth century, many people hunted caribou for their skins, which were worth a lot of money. Some herds disappeared completely. Hunting is not the only problem for caribou. People have built pipelines, or chains of pipes, to carry oil across the Arctic. These pipelines can block the caribou's migration paths. Also, too much logging, or cutting trees, is hard on the caribou that live in the taiga.

Now there are rules about how many caribou can be hunted. Many parts of the taiga are off-limits to logging. Caribou may be making a comeback!

GLOSSARY

antlers (ANT-lerz) Large branchlike horns that grow on the heads of some animals.

layer (LAY-er) One thickness of something.

lichen (LY-ken) Living things that are made of two kinds of living things, called an alga and a fungus.

mating (MAY-ting) Having to do with coming together to make babies.

mosquitoes (muh-SKEE-tohz) Flying insects that feed on the blood of animals.

protect (pruh-TEKT) To keep safe.

sleds (SLEDZ) Objects used to carry people or things across snow.

surface (SER-fes) The outside of anything.

taiga (TY-guh) A forest with fir and spruce trees, or trees that have cones and needlelike leaves, which starts where a tundra, or icy land, ends.

tame (TAYM) Made gentle or raised by people.

tundra (TUN-druh) The icy land of the coldest parts of the world.

wrestle (REH-sul) To try to force another person or animal to the ground.

yearlings (YIR-lingz) Animals that are between one and two years old.

INDEX

WEB SITES

Due to the changing nature of Internet links, PowerKids Press has developed an online list of Web sites related to the subject of this book. This site is updated regularly. Please use this link to access the list: www.powerkidslinks.com/brrr/caribou/